T0008960

THE LITTLE BOOK OF
SYDNEY

Published in 2022 by OH!
An Imprint of Welbeck Non-Fiction Limited,
part of Welbeck Publishing Group.
Based in London and Sydney.
www.welbeckpublishing.com

ISBN 978-1-80069-170-4

Compiled and written by: Drew McGovern
Editorial: Lisa Dyer
Project manager: Russell Porter
Design: punchbowldesign.com
Production: Jess Brisley

A CIP catalogue record for this book is available from the British Library

Printed in China

10 9 8 7 6 5 4 3 2 1

Cover image: biplane_desire/Shutterstock. Other images: Noch/Shutterstock

THE LITTLE BOOK OF
SYDNEY

THE WORLD'S MOST
BEAUTIFUL HARBOUR CITY AND
ICONIC ARCHITECTURE

CONTENTS

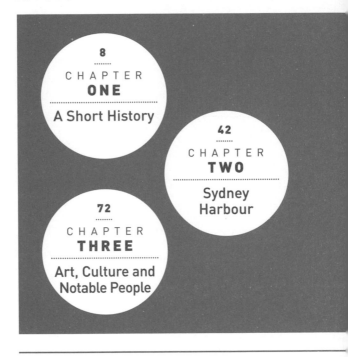

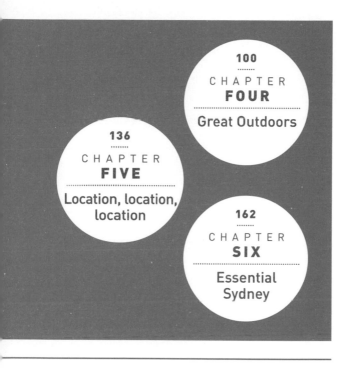

Acknowledgement

The author acknowledges the people of the Eora Nation as the traditional custodians of this place we now call Sydney, and pays his respect to the Elders past and present.

INTRODUCTION

Home to indigenous Australians for 30,000 years, Sydney itself is a relative newcomer on the global stage. Starting out as a remote British convict outpost in 1788, Sydney has since grown and reinvented herself many times to become Australia's most populous city. And with over 250 languages spoken, Sydney is also one of the world's most multicultural cities.

While the "Harbour City" is one of the most expensive places in the world to live, it often ranks among the top ten most liveable cities as well. And with year-round mild weather, numerous beaches and outdoor spaces, the magnificent harbour and a vibrant urban culture that takes full advantage of all these aspects, it's easy to see why.

There's always plenty to see and do in Sydney: catch a harbour ferry, take in a cricket match, climb the Harbour Bridge, go to a show at the Opera House, have a dip at one of the 70 beaches, join in one of the many festivals, yell yourself hoarse at a Rugby League game, take in an art exhibition or just simply find a quiet corner of the city to meditate.

It is impossible to know Sydney fully. For new visitors, returned friends and seasoned Sydneysiders alike, there is always something new to find in this ever-changing place. So when in Sydney, the best thing to do is: take a deep breath, step forward and let this amazing city introduce herself to you.

CHAPTER
ONE

A Short History

The history of Sydney begins
with the European colonization of an
ancient land and people.

In the 230 years since, Sydney
has been re-imagined multiple times
through conflicts, gold rushes, waves of
immigration, world wars, recessions
and boom times.

Traces of Sydney's history – both
indigenous and colonial – can still be
seen across the city today.

Botany Bay, in the
southern suburbs of Sydney, is
where, on 29 April 1770, Lieutenant
James Cook and the crew from
HMS *Endeavour* became the first
Europeans to make landfall on the
eastern coastline of Australia.

The Sydney area is the traditional lands of many clans, who shared a common language and kinship, called the Eora people.

Pronounced "yura", the word comes from *Ee* ("yes") and *ora* ("this place"), showing a shared identity deeply connected to the land in which they lived.

The traditional custodians of
the southern areas of Sydney,
including Botany Bay, are the
descendants of the Gweagal clan of
the Dharawal people.

Originally, Lt James Cook
called the bay of their first
landfall "Stingray Bay", but later
crossed this out and renamed
it Botany Bay because of the
unique specimens collected there
by botanists Joseph Banks and
Daniel Solander.

Botany Bay was the original destination of the First Fleet of English colonists, but upon arrival the location was quickly deemed unsuitable.

A few days later, on 26 January 1788, Captain Arthur Phillip chose a snug cove in the harbour of Port Jackson, 14km (9 miles) up the coast, to establish an English convict colony. It was to be called "New Albion", but Phillip changed his mind and called it "Sydney" instead.

66

Ithaca itself was scarcely
more longed for by
Ulysses, than Botany Bay
by the adventurers who
had traversed so many
thousand miles to take
possession of it.

99

Watkin Tench (1758–1833), British marine officer

15

Sydney

was named after
Thomas Townshend,
1st Viscount Sydney, who
was the English Home
Secretary responsible for
establishing a colony at
Botany Bay after the loss
of the American colonies
in 1776.

Gadi

is the indigenous name for Sydney Cove. The original inhabitants called themselves Gadigal (being the male form, or Gadigalleon being the female form).

The word "Gadi" comes from the name of the grass trees that used to be endemic to the area.

Six days after the First Fleet arrived in Botany Bay, two ships of the French explorer Lapérouse (*Astrolabe* and *Boussole*) sailed into the bay. The Sydney suburb of La Perouse along the north headland at the entrance to Botany Bay bears his name.

Soon after arrival, the chaplain of the *Astrolabe* died from injuries sustained in Samoa. He was buried ashore at a location now called Frenchman's Cove.

The First Fleet

consisted of 11 ships, including
two Royal Navy ships, six convict
transports and three store ships.

Accounts vary, but it is thought
that approximately 1,500 people
reached Sydney Cove.

The first census of Sydney was made by Governor Phillip in 1788. In his report to Lord Sydney, the British population of the colony was listed as 1,030.

There were also 7 horses, 7 cows, 74 pigs, 29 sheep and 6 rabbits.

Before the arrival
of the European settlers, the
indigenous population around
the Sydney region was
estimated at between 4,000
and 8,000 people from as
many as 29 clans.

Tank Stream

was a spring-fed freshwater stream that flowed down to the harbour shore between present-day George and Pitt Streets.

Its existence was the primary reason Arthur Phillip chose this site for the first European settlement and not anywhere else in Port Jackson.

66

Into the head of the cove,
on which our establishment
is fixed, runs a small stream
of fresh water, which serves
to divide the adjacent country
to a little distance, in the
direction of north and south.

99

Watkin Tench (1758–1833), British marine officer

Bungaree

Originally from Broken Bay, north of Sydney, Bungaree was a popular well-known Aboriginal man from the 1790s until his death in 1830. He was a charismatic, witty and intelligent diplomat welcomed in both indigenous and settler societies.

He had an adventurous spirit and accompanied Matthew Flinders on his circumnavigation of Australia in 1803, becoming the first Australian to sail round the continent.

In 1815 Governor Macquarie established an "experimental" farm for him and about 16 other Aboriginals on Middle Head. Macquarie also dubbed Bungaree "King of Port Jackson".

Bugaree was the first Australian to be recorded in print and, later in life, was renowned as an entertainer and a cultural educator.

He is commemorated in Rose Bay by a terraced garden called Bungaree Reserve.

Colonial Governors of New South Wales

Captain Arthur Phillip, RN 1788–1792
Captain John Hunter, RN 1795–1800
Captain Philip Gidley King, RN 1800–1806
Captain William Bligh, RN 1806–1808
MG Lachlan Macquarie 1810–1821
MG Sir Thomas Brisbane 1821–1825
Lt-Gen. Ralph Darling 1825–1831
MG Sir Richard Bourke 1831–1837
Sir George Gipps 1838–1846
Sir Charles FitzRoy 1846–1855
Sir William Denison 1855–1861
Rt Hon. Sir John Young 1861–1867
Rt Hon. Somerset Lowry-Corry 1868–1872
Sir Hercules Robinson 1872–1879
Rt Hon. Lord Augustus Loftus 1879–1885
Rt Hon. Charles Carrington 1885–1890
Rt Hon. Victor Child Villiers 1891–1893
Rt Hon. Sir Robert Duff 1893–1895
Rt Hon. Henry Robert Brand 1895–1899
Rt Hon. William Beauchamp 1899–1901

When gold was discovered in 1851, one of the many nationalities to join the gold rush was the Chinese. By 1855 there were 17,000 Chinese people in Sydney, some of whom set up businesses in The Rocks.

By the 1920s, the "Chinese Quarter" had moved to Haymarket, where Chinatown is located today.

James Squire (the namesake of a popular Sydney-based brewing company) was a convict who arrived in 1788 with the First Fleet. While it is uncertain that he was the first person to brew beer in Australia, Squire certainly was the first to successfully grow hops.

In 1798, he established the Malting Shovel Inn on the Parramatta River. Halfway between the two main settlements of the colony, his watering hole proved popular with sailors wanting to wait for the tide to turn.

Sydney Gazette

*The Sydney Gazette and
New South Wales Advertiser*
was the first newspaper printed
in the early colony between
1803 and 1843.

It was printed on a small
second-hand printing press that
came over with the First Fleet.

The first highway in
Australia between two cities is
Parramatta Road, which opened
in 1811 and linked the cities of
Sydney and Parramatta.

Three men, Blaxland, Wentworth
and Lawson, probably following
Aboriginal trails, were the first
settlers to cross the Blue Mountains
in 1813, opening up the inland
regions to pastoralism.

Sydney would soon benefit by being
a lucrative centre of the colonial
wool trade with Britain.

The Rum Rebellion

of 1808 was the only successful *coup d'état* in Australian history.

Governor William Bligh (yes, the hapless captain from the mutiny on the *Bounty*) was up against the powerful Rum Corps – the military officers running Sydney's illicit rum trade. Bligh had been in office less than two years before the military arrested him and took control of the colony until the 1810 arrival of Major-General Lachlan Macquarie, who became the colony's new governor.

In 1802, the first book
published in Australia was
New South Wales Standing Orders.
It was printed by George Howe,
who had worked as a printer before
being sentenced to transportation
for shoplifting in 1799.

Howe was also the first editor of the
Sydney Gazette in 1803.

Gold Rush!

In 1851, a gold rush began near Bathurst, west of Sydney, by Edward Hargraves, who had only just returned from the Californian gold fields. The influx of people and wealth to the colony changed Sydney's economy for ever.

Within 10 years, the population had increased by 78%. Modern Sydney had arrived!

In June 1942, three midget submarines of the Imperial Japanese Navy entered the harbour and attempted to sink Allied warships.

Two of the midget subs were detected and sunk before they could attack. A third attempted to torpedo heavy cruiser USS *Chicago* but instead sunk the converted ferry HMAS *Kuttabul*, killing 21 sailors.

"

All the wealth in the world
could not purchase the
self-respect which had been
cut out of him by the lash,
or banish from his brain the
memory of his degradation.

"

Marcus Clarke (1846–1881), referring to
Rufus Dawes, a character in his novel, *For the Term of
His Natural Life* (1874), who was wrongfully
transported to Australia as a convict.

In 1900 an epidemic of the
bubonic plague broke out in
Sydney. With its close proximity
to the dockyards, The Rocks
area was blamed as the source
of contagion.

However, of the 303 cases
recorded, only five were from
The Rocks.

Western and southwestern Sydney is a diverse fabric of cultures, languages, religions and incomes. The post-war boom era saw Sydney expand westward to the open spaces.

First-generation Australians and inner-city working-class residents, seeking a better life for themselves, found a new home in Western Sydney.

Before closing down in 1961,
Sydney's extensive tram network
was the largest in Australia and the
second largest in the British
Commonwealth after London.

At its height in the 1930s, there were
about 1,600 cars in active service.
The growth in private car ownership in
the 1950s saw the decline of
tram passenger numbers.

The Sydney Morning Herald is a mainstay of many Sydneysiders' daily breakfast routine.

Founded in 1831, *The Herald* – as it is affectionately known – is Australia's oldest continually published newspaper.

This is really
a wonderful Colony;
ancient Rome, in her
Imperial grandeur, would
not have been ashamed
of such an offspring.

Charles Darwin (1809–1882), naturalist

CHAPTER
TWO

Sydney Harbour

In 1788, a British colony was established in a tiny cove they called "Sydney". In the story of how the colony evolved into a city, the harbour has been the central character of every chapter.

Geographically, Port Jackson is a submerged coastal valley. Culturally, however, this beautiful body of water has always been the life blood of Sydney.

Sydney Harbour ... one of the finest, most beautiful, vast and safe bays the sun had ever shone upon.

Joseph Conrad (1857–1924), Polish-British writer

Lighthouses of Sydney

Bradleys Head Lighthouse – 1905
Bradleys Head, Mosman

Dawes Point Lighthouse – 1905 (rebuilt 1946)
Hickson Road, Circular Quay

Grotto Point Lighthouse – 1911
Lighthouse Track, Balgowlah Heights

Henry Head Lighthouse – 1955
La Perouse, Port Botany

Hornby Lighthouse – 1858
South Head, Watsons Bay

Robertson Point Lighthouse – 1910
Athol Wharf Road, Cremorne Point

Barrenjoey Lighthouse – 1881
Barrenjoey Road, Palm Beach

Cape Baily Lighthouse – 1950
Cape Baily Track, Kurnell

Macquarie Lighthouse – 1883
Old South Head Road, Vaucluse

The Manly Ferry

is Sydney's most famous harbour ferry. The service began life in 1853 when Henry Gilbert Smith chartered a paddle wheeler to promote his property subdivision, near the Corso, by bringing Sydneysiders to Manly. It soon became a popular beachside destination, and by 1859, the first double-ended ferry, *Phantom*, began regular services.

The Sydney
Harbour Bridge
is often
affectionately
nicknamed
"The Coathanger".

The iconic arch design of the Sydney Harbour Bridge is a combination of the Tyne Bridge in Newcastle-upon-Tyne in England and Hell Gate Bridge in New York City.

Gadigal Country

The area of land along southern
Sydney Harbour, from
Darling Harbour to the eastern
beaches including South Head,
is the traditional lands of the
Gadigal people.

Middle Head

A place of enduring significance for the Borogegal people, this peninsular has a spectacular view of Sydney Harbour and the seaway entrance.

Despite Sydney's remote location on the globe, defensive gun emplacements were built in response to perceived distant threats: in 1801 for the Napoleonic Wars and in 1871 to defend against Russian attack. But during World War II, the threat was closer to home when Japanese midget subs were found in Sydney Harbour. Throughout this time however, the guns were never fired in anger.

In other times, the headland has been an Aboriginal farming community established by Governor Macquarie, freehold farmland, a golf course and, finally, a national park.

66

... there is material for a
dozen buccaneering stories
to be picked up in the
hotels at Circular Quay.

99

**Robert Louis Stevenson (1850–1894),
Scottish novelist**

The largest island in Sydney Harbour is

Cockatoo Island.

Since European settlement, it has been a prison, a dockyard and a ship-building facility.

Today visitors can catch a ferry from Circular Quay to go on guided tours, engage in sporting activities, take in an opera and even stay overnight.

Harbour Bridge by numbers

Eighth longest-spanning arch bridge in the world at 503m (1,650ft)

Tallest steel arch bridge: 134m (440ft) from water level to the top of the arch

Second widest long-span bridge in the world: 48.8m (160ft)

Contains 6 million hand-driven rivets

Weighs 52,800 tonnes

The pylons are 89m (292ft) high

Sydney Harbour Ferry Routes

All ferry routes on Sydney Harbour leave from Circular Quay. Here is a list of the route numbers and their terminus locations:

F1 Manly

F2 Taronga Zoo

F3 Parramatta River

F4 Pyrmont Bay

F5 Neutral Bay

F6 Mosman Bay

F7 Double Bay

F8 Cockatoo Island

F9 Watsons Bay

Since June 2001, jet skis have been banned on Sydney Harbour, Parramatta River and Lane Cove River.

Fort Denison was known to the indigenous population as Mat-te-wan-ye. The low-lying island with the tiny stone fort you can see today was originally a 15m (49ft)-high outcrop of sandstone.

The island was quarried to construct Circular Quay – reducing the overall height to a platform only a few metres above water level.

Circular Quay

has been the beating
heart of the harbour since
the initial landing in Sydney
Cove by Arthur Phillip
in 1788, and is often
referred to as "the Gateway
to Sydney".

"

Rock pools, so-named because they have been hammered out of rocks at the ocean's edge, are one of Sydney's defining characteristics, along with the Opera House and Harbour Bridge, though not as well known.

"

Raymond Bonner, American author and investigative reporter

The first ferry on Sydney Harbour is considered to be the *Rose Hill Packet*, built within a year of the First Fleet.

Nicknamed "The Lump", it was an ungainly vessel that carried goods and passengers between Circular Quay and Rose Hill (Parramatta).

Sydney Harbour by numbers

Including all of Port Jackson, from the gap between North and South Head to the Paramatta River.

317km (197 miles) of shoreline

55sq km (34sq miles) of water surface

19km (12 miles) long

562 million cubic meters
(1844 million cubic feet) of water

8 islands

20 headlands and peninsulas

7 tributaries and waterways

13 bridges

1 cable ferry

1 weir

Manly.
Seven miles from Sydney and a thousand miles from care.

Advertising slogan dating from the 1920s to encourage
Sydneysiders to use the Manly Ferry

Sydney Harbour is a unit of measure in itself. A Sydharb (or sydarb) is equivalent to 500 gigalitres (410,000 acre ft). For instance, Melbourne's Port Philip Bay holds an equivalent volume of 50 Sydharbs.

Sydney to Hobart Yacht Race

Since the inaugural race in 1945 with only nine boats, the Sydney to Hobart Yacht Race has grown to become one of the top three ocean races in the world.

The 1,170km (630 nautical miles) from Sydney Harbour to Constitution Dock in Hobart, Tasmania is a gruelling testing ground for any would-be champion sailor.

The roadway across the Sydney Harbour Bridge is called the Bradfield Highway.

At just 2.4km (1.5 miles) long, it is one of Australia's shortest highways.

One of the best locations to take in harbour views is

Bradleys Head.

On the North Shore of the harbour, you can look across to the Opera House, the CBD (city centre) and the Harbour Bridge. It's also a great place to enjoy the New Year's Eve fireworks display – but you'll have to get there super early to reserve your spot!

Rose Bay Water Airport started life in 1938 as a flying boat base where passengers could board flights bound for London. This made it Sydney's first international airport.

Today, it's a great place to catch a bird's-eye view of the harbour on one of the sightseeing flights.

66

In Sydney Harbour ... the yachts will be racing on the crushed diamond water under a sky the texture of powdered sapphires. It would be churlish not to concede that the same abundance of natural blessings which gave us the energy to leave has every right to call us back.

99

Clive James (1939–2019), *Unreliable Memoirs* (1980)

First Fleet ferries

Of the 42 ferries plying the waters of Sydney Harbour, there is a fleet of nine First Fleet class catamaran ferries that are all named after the ships of the "First Fleet".

Sirius

Supply

Alexander

Borrowdale

Charlotte

Fishburn

Friendship

Golden Grove

Scarborough

There are two tunnels under the harbour linking the north to the south. The Sydney Harbour Tunnel was completed in 1992 to help alleviate road traffic on the Harbour Bridge.

The other subterranean crossing (due for completion in 2024) is part of the Sydney Metro, an automated rapid transit rail line.

Sydney Rock Oysters

Sydneysiders have a deep love of their local oysters. The indigenous people feasted on them regularly and the European settlers were no different. The shells were burnt to produce lime for mortar used in the construction of the early colony.

So, you could say Sydney Rock Oysters are in the very fabric of the city!

The views of the Opera House and Harbour Bridge from

Mrs Macquarie's Chair

make this one of the best vantage points on the harbour. Hand-carved into exposed sandstone rock in 1810, the chair sits on a peninsula known to the Gadigal people as Yurong.

With views like this, Sydney Harbour is your rock oyster!

CHAPTER
THREE

Art, Culture and Notable People

It could be said that Sydney wears its heart on its sleeve. Sometimes meditative, sometimes chaotic, sometimes just plain rude, but never dull, Sydney is a truly interactive city.

This is reflected no more so than in the people who have made their mark on the city and the work that they create.

"

One of the great things about Sydney is that it has a great acceptance of everyone and everything. It's an incredibly tolerant city, a city with a huge multicultural basis.

"

Baz Luhrmann, director, writer and producer

Sydney's 45.5%
foreign-born
population ranks third
largest in the world
after London and New
York City.

Few things express the powerful zeitgeist of Sydney's coming-of-age during the 1970s and '80s more than

Flamingo Park Frock Salon.

Designers Jenny Kee and Linda Jackson rejected the stogy cultural cringe of the times and lovingly embraced "kitsch Australiana". Suddenly, Flamingo Park gave Australian fashion an "explosion of shape and colour" and a newfound presence on the world stage.

Bangarra
Dance Theatre

Bangarra is an Aboriginal and Torres Strait Islander contemporary performing arts company founded in 1989. All of the company's dancers have proud indigenous heritage. Acclaimed nationally and around the world, Bangarra's distinctive repertoire comes from a deep connection to the people of the Eora Nation and stories handed on from respected community Elders.

Born in Sydney in 1887, Annette Kellermann was one of the first women in the early 1900s to wear a one-piece bathing costume.
She advocated for the right of women to wear less cumbersome bathing costumes and developed her own line of swimwear following the popularity of her one-piece suits.

Kellermann went on to become the first woman to appear nude in a Hollywood film, and has her own star on the Walk of Fame.

The Museum of Contemporary Art

was opened in 1991 with the intention of making contemporary art and ideas widely accessible.

Located on the western side of Circular Quay, and housed in the Art Deco grandeur of the former Maritime Services building, the MCA welcomes over a million visitors each year.

Bennelong

Woollarawarre Bennelong was a Wangal man from the southern banks of the Parramatta River. He was abducted, with another Aboriginal man, by English soldiers in 1790. He soon escaped captivity and actively resisted the colonists for about a year, before eventually becoming friends with Governor Phillip. A skilled politician, Bennelong quickly learned English and mediated between the indigenous and European cultures.

At this time, Bennelong Point, the site of the Sydney Opera House, was named after him by Governor Phillip.

In 1792, Bennelong, along with another Aboriginal man, sailed with Governor Phillip to England where they both met with English society and possibly King George III. When his companion died of a chest infection, Bennelong returned to Sydney, becoming the first Aboriginal man to visit Europe and return.

It is said that having seen the best and worst of European culture, Bennelong rejected it and left the colony to return to the bush and his people. He died in 1813 and was buried in the orchard of his friend, the brewer James Squire, along the banks of the Parramatta River.

Major Sydney Art Galleries

Sydney boasts a multitude of art galleries, from small, independently run initiatives to major establishments. Below is a short list of the major art galleries of Sydney showcasing up-and-coming, contemporary and classic art exhibitions and events throughout the year.

Museum of Contemporary Art – The Rocks

Art Gallery of NSW – The Domain

The Artery Contemporary Aboriginal Art Gallery – Darlinghurst

White Rabbit Gallery – Chippendale

Carriageworks – Redfern

Casula Powerhouse Arts Centre – Casula, Southwestern Sydney

66

Sydney in the 1960s wasn't the exuberant multicultural metropolis it is today. Out in the city's western reaches, days passed in a sun-struck stupor. In the evenings, families gathered on their verandas waiting for the 'southerly buster' – the thunderstorm that would break the heat and leave the air cool enough to allow sleep.

99

Geraldine Brooks, Sydney-born journalist and novelist

Skippy the Bush Kangaroo

was a popular Australian TV series produced in the late 1960s. It follows the adventures of a young boy and an unusually intelligent kangaroo. Set in the fictional Waratah National Park on the traditional lands of the Guringai people just inland from Sydney's northern beaches, the show became one of Australia's most exported TV programmes.

Mr Eternity

From the 1930s to the 1960s, Arthur Stace wrote his one-word sermon, "Eternity", in yellow chalk on the sidewalks of Sydney. Becoming a folklore legend in the process, his identity remained unknown until 1956.

There is a wrought aluminium replica of "Eternity", set in Stace's famous copperplate script, in the pavement near the waterfall of Town Hall Square in the CBD.

Since 1921, the Art Gallery of New South Wales has hosted the annual

Archibald Prize.

It is Australia's best known portraiture art prize for painting. The winner, often a controversial topic of discussion across the nation, is awarded $100,000. The People's Choice Award chosen by the general public and the Packing Room Prize are alternative prizes also given out. Never has an artist won all three at the same time.

Home and Away

Set in the fictional seaside town of
Summer Bay, this long-running
Australian soap opera first aired in
January 1988. Sold to over 80 countries
worldwide, it is one of Australia's most
successful media exports.

Exterior scenes are filmed mainly at
Palm Beach and Fisherman's Beach
on Sydney's northern beaches.
For fans of the show, they can join one
of the tours of the film sets.

It's difficult to imagine growing up in Sydney, and not going to

Royal Easter Show.

Held over two weeks around Easter, the event combines a trade fair, an amusement park and an agricultural show. The result is a delightfully chaotic assault on the senses – much-loved by Sydneysiders.

A true signature of Sydney, it is Australia's largest annual ticketed event, attracting about 828,000 visitors each year.

What started in 1978 as part
of a commemoration of the 1969
Stonewall riots in New York,

the Sydney Gay and
Lesbian Mardi Gras

has grown to become one of the
biggest Pride events in the world today.
Besides the famous street parade,
there are fairs, harbour parties,
discussion panels, award ceremonies
and film festivals held in venues
across the city.

66

On hot nights before
the nor'easter came
you changed into your
cossie and ran under the
sprinkler.

99

Clive James (1939–2019), *Unreliable Memoirs* **(1980)**

Vivid Sydney

is a festival of light, music and ideas held every winter. It began in 2009 as an energy-efficient light festival. Since then, the festival has grown to feature interactive multimedia, light sculptures, building projections, music gigs and forum events.

At night the Opera House, Harbour Bridge, the CBD and The Rocks become canvases for projected art and huge multimedia works.

66

When I have a
bad day, I dream about
opening up a gelato stand
on the streets of Sydney,
Australia. Doesn't
everyone have a random
escape fantasy?

99

Nancy Lublin, social enterprise entrepreneur

Thomas Keneally is an Australian Living Treasure.

A prolific Sydney novelist, playwright, essayist and actor, his novel *Schindler's Ark* (winner of the Booker Prize in 1982) was adapted into the movie *Schindler's List*.

The founding chairman of the Australian Republic Movement, he is also a keen supporter of the Manly-Warringah Sea Eagles Rugby League club.

If you're in Sydney in January, you won't be able to miss the

Sydney Festival.

With over 100 events – a number of them free, large-scale outdoor events – involving local and international acts and classical and contemporary dance, music, drama, circus and visual arts, as well as artist talks, Sydneysiders and visitors are spoiled for choice.

"High Rise" Harry

In a city obsessed by property development, Harry Triguboff looms large in Sydney's psyche.

The billionaire founder of Meriton built his first block of units in 1963 – starting a career spanning over 50 years.

By 2015, he is said to have built around 55,000 residential units and apartments.

Australian comedy duo
Greig Pickhaver (as H. G. Nelson)
and John Doyle (as Rampaging Roy
Slaven) hosted *This Sporting Life*,
a live-to-air satirical radio sports
programme.

Combining a love of sport with
irreverent lampooning, the Saturday
radio show was a staple of Sydney's
weekends from 1986 to 2008.

The comedic characters also made
appearances as sportscasters for
major events such as the 2000 Sydney
Olympics – to great acclaim.

> # The sort of weekend where too much sport is barely enough!

An often-quoted line from the introduction monologue for *This Sporting Life*, read by voice-over presenter Robbie McGregor playing "King Wally Otto in the Soundproof Booth".

Tropfest

is a short film festival where all the movies must be made specifically for the event. The short films should also run less than seven minutes, including credits, and have their world premiere at Tropfest.

What began informally among friends in 1993 at the Tropicana Caffe in Darlinghurst now has events held in Berlin, London, Bangkok, Toronto, New York City, Japan, Africa and the Middle East.

An incomplete list of Sydney recording artists

Alex Lloyd

Angus & Julia Stone

The Aztecs

Baby Animals

Ben Lee

Bliss N Eso

Boy & Bear

The Church

Col Joye

The Cruel Sea

Divinyls

The Easybeats

Empire of the Sun

Flume

Frenzal Rhomb

Hoodoo Gurus

INXS

James Morrison

Johnny O'Keefe

Midnight Oil

Natalie Imbruglia

The Presets

Radio Birdman

Rick Springfield

Rose Tattoo

Sarah Blasko

The Vines

Wolfmother

You Am I

CHAPTER
FOUR

Great Outdoors

Sydney certainly holds bragging rights for some of the best weather in the world. Glorious summers and relatively mild winters mean Sydneysiders are quite familiar with outdoor pursuits.

Whether partaking in an organized sport or spectating at a athletic event, going to the beach or simply taking a walk, in Sydney there's no need to stay at home.

"

The best things about Sydney are free: the sunshine's free, and the harbour's free, and the beach is free.

"

Russell Crowe, actor, director, musician and singer

Bondi was the first beach in Australia to legalize daylight bathing in 1902.

It was also the first beach to establish a surf lifesavers club five years later, owing to the exploding popularity of sea bathing.

In the southeastern pylon of Sydney Harbour Bridge you'll find amuseum, a tourist centre and, at the top, a 360° lookout with spectacular views over the harbour, the Opera House and the CBD.

Hyde Park

Named by Governor Macquarie after the famous park in London, this 16 hectare (40 acre) area in the heart of central Sydney was formally reserved for public use in 1810, making it the first public park in Australia.

Until it was dedicated as public gardens in 1856, Hyde Park was a racecourse and the venue of the first organized horse race in Australia.

Centennial Park,

"the People's Park", was established in 1888 to commemorate Australia's centenary.

It was opened by Sir Henry Parkes – a prominent politician often referred to as the "Father of Federation" for his work in promoting the federation of the six colonies of Australia.

In 1901, five years after Parkes' death, Centennial Park was the site of the inauguration of the Commonwealth of Australia.

Established in 1816,

the Royal Botanic Garden

is Australia's oldest scientific institution. Originally, the 30 hectare (74 acre) site at Farm Cove was Australia's first farm established by Europeans in 1788.

Today it's a hive of activity, with events, courses, markets and more – all available to the public.

"

If Paris is a city of lights, Sydney is the city of fireworks.

"

Baz Luhrmann, director, writer and producer

Inspired by the Brooklyn Bridge
100th anniversary fireworks in 1983,
the Sydney Harbour Bridge is the
focal point for the

New Year's Eve
fireworks.

In 2010/11 it was reported that
1.5 million people watched on from
the harbour and a further 1.1 billion
tuned in globally.

It is calculated that 25.9% of Sydney is covered by trees, making Sydney the third largest city in the world with the most trees.

Watching the start of the
Sydney to Hobart Yacht Race
is a Boxing Day tradition.

Sydneysiders by their hundreds
of thousands, lining the harbour
shoreline or afloat on spectator
boats, come out to see which of the
maxi-yachts will be first out
through the heads.

With quite a carnival atmosphere,
it's a great day out.

Spectacular views of Sydney can be had from the observation deck of

Sydney Tower.

A member of the World Federation of Great Towers, it is 305m (1,001 ft) tall, being the tallest structure in Sydney.

Open to the public, the turret also offers revolving restaurants and bars – all with 360º views. And for the truly adventurous, Skywalk is a glass-floored viewing platform around the *outside* of the turret 268m (879ft) above the ground.

For a slow, intimate experience
of the harbour foreshore, the

Bondi to Manly Walk

is just the ticket. A series of well-made
tracks that hug the shoreline allows
walkers to go from Bondi to Manly via
the Harbour Bridge.

Take in ocean views, quiet bays, the
noisy cityand Aboriginal sites along
the way. At 80km (50 miles) one way,
it's best broken into day trips. Luckily,
there's a smartphone app that can help
you plan your walks.

Using an indigenous word meaning "beautiful view",

Taronga Zoo

sure lives up to its name. Set on elevated land, most of the park has spectacular harbour views.

It's a great day out, but you can also stay the night. Accommodation is available inside the park, complete with tours and strange noises at night.

There are
70 beaches
along Sydney's
coastline.

66

I think Sydney has so much natural beauty; it's just a beautiful city.

99

Flume, Australian musician, DJ and record producer

On 26 January, Sydney Harbour
comes alive for the iconic

Ferrython.

A small fleet of ferries race from
Barangaroo Wharf to Shark Island
and then finish back under the Sydney
Harbour Bridge. The event can be
viewed free from any of the harbour
vantage points around the bridge.

You can also join in the fun. A ticket
on one of the competing ferries will get
you drinks, lunch and bragging
rights if you win.

The riot that ended in Ashes

Passions have always run deep with Sydneysiders and Test cricket. None so more than in 1879, when a riot erupted at the Sydney Cricket Ground.

Australia was playing a touring English team when a questionable umpiring decision went against the Australian batsman hero Billy Murdoch. Emotions boiled over and 2,000 spectators invaded the pitch, assaulting the umpire and some English players.

118

All of England was, of course, appalled. From that point on, the rivalry was personal. In 1882, Australia's first win on English soil prompted an obituary in a British newspaper, mourning the death of English cricket and telling readers that "the body will be cremated and the ashes taken to Australia". The following season, the English captain stated they were playing to "regain the ashes".

To this day, when Australia and England play Test cricket, they are still playing for *The Ashes*.

Until 1902,
swimming at any of
Sydney's beaches
during daylight hours
was against the law.

66

I basically sat around unemployed in Sydney for three years straight, and the two things that saved me were the Rugby League and my dog.

99

Ben Mendelsohn, Australian actor

Winter Swimming Clubs

Swimming is a popular pastime for Sydneysiders, even during the winter months, as these Sydney winter swimming clubs attest to.

Cronulla Polar Bears
Winter Swimming Club

South Maroubra Dolphins
Winter Swimming Club

Clovelly Eskimos
Winter Swimming Club

Maroubra Seals
Winter Swimming Club

Coogee Penguins
Winter Swimming Club

Bronte Splashers

The Bondi Icebergs
Winter Swimming Club

Bondi to Coogee Walk

This is probably Sydney's most popular walk. With ocean views, Waverly Cemetery, secluded coves, swimming beaches, dramatic cliffs, cafés, pubs, drinking fountains and toilets along an easy 6km (3.7 mile) path, it's easy to see why.

Rides at Luna Park

Below is a list of the permanent rides at Luna Park as of 2020. During peak times, extra fun-fair rides are contracted to operate.

Hair Raiser – a 50m (160ft)-drop tower

Wild Mouse – roller coaster

Ferris Wheel – 35 metres (56 ft) tall

Rotor – rotating gravity ride

The Carousel – classic carousel ride

Volaré – Australia's largest swing chair ride

Dodgem City – 19-car dodgem hall

Tango Train II – caterpillar ride

South Sydney
Rabbitohs Rugby League
team is part-owned
by Hollywood star
Russell Crowe, himself
a long-time member
of the club.

First held in 1971, the

City2Surf

is a 14km (8.7 mile) fun run and race where the 80,000 participants start in the city centre and try to finish at Bondi Beach. At the halfway mark, runners meet the infamous "Heartbreak Hill", a 2km (1.2 mile) steep climb that has claimed many an aspiring runner.

The course records are 40:03 minutes, set by Steve Moneghetti in 1991, and 45:08 minutes, set by Susie Power in 2001.

Ironpeople

At surf lifesaving carnivals around Australia, the Ironman and Ironwoman events always draw a crowd.

Combining the four disciplines of surf lifesaving (swimming, board paddling, ski padding and running), champions of this gruelling event often become household names and appear on breakfast cereal boxes.

Narrabeen Beach

is mentioned in the lyrics
of The Beach Boys'
hit single "Surfing USA".

The Great Aussie Cossie

In 1927, Sydney underwear manufacturer MacRae and Company Hosiery released their first "racer-back" swimming costume line. In a competition held among staff to name this new line of garments, Captain Parsonson won £5 for his slogan "Speed on in your Speedos".

And just like that, the world-famous Speedo sports brand was born!

It's difficult to imagine Sydney without her beloved

Rugby League.

Imported in 1908, this British breakaway form of rugby was seen as the sport for the working classes.

Within a few seasons, Rugby League had displaced traditional Rugby Union and established Sydney as Australia's epicentre of the football code so loved by workers, artists, politicians and poets.

Established in 1877,

Waverly Cemetery

covers 16 hectares (40 acres) with over 50,000 grave sites perched on a clifftop overlooking the ocean.

Join a walking tour and discover the largest memorial to Irish rebels outside of Ireland, the graves of soldiers who fought in the American War of Independence and many other interesting stories.

The dangers of rowing a boat through crashing surf cannot be overstated.

Surf boat crew are usually the wild larrikins of surf clubs. As the old joke goes: to choose the boat crew, surf club members would be lined up and have house bricks thrown at them. Those members who didn't duck were chosen for the surf boat event.

Shelly Beach at Manly is one of only two west-facing ocean beaches on the Australian east coast.

18-Footers

Fast, colourful and glamorous, the 18ft sailing skiff is the quintessential Sydney harbour sailing class. Started in 1892 to add excitement to the sport of sailing, the "18-footers" have evolved to become the high-tech sailing craft of today.

With many vantage points around the harbour, and sightseeing chartered ferry boats, the 18-footers are a must-see spectator sport for any sailing enthusiast.

Sydney-based sporting teams

Greater Western Sydney Giants – AFL

Sydney Swans – AFL

Greater Western Sydney Giants – Netball

New South Wales Swifts – Netball

New South Wales Blues – Cricket

Sydney Sixers – Cricket

Sydney Thunder – Cricket

New South Wales Waratahs – Rugby Union

New South Wales Waratahs – Field Hockey

Sydney Blue Sox – Baseball

Sydney FC – Football

Western Sydney Wanderers FC – Football

Sydney Kings – Basketball

Sydney Uni Flames – Women's Basketball

Sydney Bears – Ice Hockey

Sydney Ice Dogs – Ice Hockey

CHAPTER
FIVE

Location, location, location

Sydney has some unique geography.

The habour, cutting through
the middle, defines north and south,
the ocean marking the east, and
the mountains to the west.

Within the city boundaries, every
building, street, suburb and region has
its own unique part to play in
Sydney's character.

Indigenous clans of Sydney

Below are some of the clans around greater Sydney at the time of European colonization.

The Kuring-gai
(northern Sydney around Broken Bay)

The Dharawal
(the head of the Paramatta River)

The Comma or Canna
(Middle Harbour from Clontarf to Manly)

The Wangal
(the southern shores of the Parramatta River)

The Wallumattagal
(the north shore between Milsons Point and Lane Cove)

The Gweagal
(the southern shores of Botany Bay and the Cronulla-Sutherland Peninsula)

The Regions of Sydney

CBD or **City of Sydney**
(colloquially referred to as "the City")

Inner West

Eastern Suburbs

South Sydney

The Shire
(including St George and Sutherland Shire)

Greater Western Sydney
(including South Western Sydney, Hills District
and the Macarthur Region)

Northern Sydney
(including the North Shore and
Northern Beaches)

66

South Sydney is a very
complicated and wonderful
place. You have some of
the most expensive bits of real
estate in the country and
a large percentage
of government housing.

99

Russell Crowe,
actor, director, musician and singer

Until 1975, Sydney had
a building height limit of 279m (915ft).
This was to allow for flying boats
on Sydney Harbour. By the 1970s,
however, the modern jet era had well
and truly arrived.

The last flying boat flew out of
Sydney in 1974.

The Inner West suburb of

Balmain

is the traditional heartland of
Australian working-class culture.
Originally a heavily industrialized area,
close to the wharfs, Balmain was
where the Australian trade unionist
movement began and the birthplace of
the Australian Labor Party.

Since the 1990s, gradual gentrification
has softened the edges somewhat
and increased property values.

142

> **"**
> There are only
> two types of men in this
> world: those who were
> born in Balmain
> and those who wish
> they were.
> **"**

Police Commissioner of New South Wales,
date unknown

Conspicuous as it is iconic,
Sydney's most
famous building, the

Sydney Opera House

holds pride of place on
Bennelong Point.

The design of the famous curved roof lines echoes the sailing boats on the harbour, and was the winning entry from Danish architect Jørn Utzon in an international design competition held in 1957. However, the structure wasn't completed until 1973.

The project was 1,357% over budget and 10 years late, but you won't hear any Sydneysiders complaining.

Built in 1855,
Kirribilli House
is situated on the North Shore
(the traditional lands of the Gamaragal
people) directly across the harbour
from the CBD.

Since the 1920s, it has been
the official Sydney residence of the
Prime Minister of Australia and
is open to the public one day a year
(usually in May).

Sydney's
Luna Park
was built under the shadow of the bridge in 1935 and has been entertaining Sydneysiders and visitors almost continuously ever since.

During that time, the enormous smiling face entrance – cheekily grinning across the harbour towards the CBD – has been changed eight times.

Known as Tallawoladah by the Gadigal people,

The Rocks

is the unlevelled rocky headland tucked under the southern end of Sydney Harbour Bridge. During the 1800s it was Sydney's melting pot of immigrants and maritime workers.

Gentrification in the late 20th century transformed it into Sydney's historic tourist precinct, where at least two pubs in the area claim to be Sydney's oldest.

148

Elizabeth Farm

in the suburb of Rose Hill is Sydney's (and Australia's) oldest building.

John Macarthur, an ambitious military officer who would later become a wealthy land owner, built the house in 1793. The historic home is open to the public as a museum.

Blues Point Tower, located on McMahons Point, is considered by some to be the ugliest building in Sydney. Until 1970, it was also Australia's tallest residential building.

Once known as Long Cove,

Darling Harbour

was renamed after Lieutenant-General Ralph Darling, the new South Wales Governor from 1825 to 1831.

Originally a major part of the port of Sydney with a railway goods yard, it was redeveloped in the 1980s into the recreational precinct it is today.

Lord Nelson Brewery Hotel

Sydney's oldest continually licensed hotel, "The Lord" was established by William Wells in 1841. He had built a two-storey house in 1836 on the corner of Kent and Argyle Streets, using sandstone blocks quarried nearby.

In 1841, Wells obtained a liquor licence for his house, and called it The Lord Nelson.

The suburbs north of the harbour are colloquially called **the North Shore.** Physically isolated by the waters of the harbour from the more populated southern shore, the rugged North Shore landscape was not developed until the Sydney Harbour Bridge opened in 1932.

Some of Sydney's original place names

Bondi: water breaking over rocks

Cabramatta: fresh tasty water grub

Coogee: smelly place (from rotten seaweed)

Cronulla: place of the small pink seashells

Dee Why: from a bird common to the area

Kirribilli: good fishing spot

Maroubra: sound of thunder (crashing surf)

Parramatta: place of eels

Woolloomooloo: place of plenty

"

... their confidence and manly behaviour made me give the name of Manly Cove to this place.

"

Captain Arthur Phillip (1738–1814),
Founding Governor of the Colony of New South Wales,
commenting after meeting the men of the
Kay-ye-my clan in Manly Cove

Queen Victoria Building

Affectionately known as QVB, this elaborate shopping arcade was restored to its Federation glory in the 1980s. Built during a severe recession in 1898, the decorative Romanesque design was also intended to employ as many out-of-work craftsmen as possible.

So not only is QVB a monument to the long-reigning monarch, it's also a fitting tribute to the stonemasons, plasterers and stained-glass-window artists as well.

Sydney's
North Shore is
the traditional lands
of the Gorualgal
and Cammeraygal
people.

"

...bottle-ohs, limousines,
paupers' funerals, police patrols,
millionaires, American actresses,
mysterious screams, and people
who don't pay their taxi-fares.
It is a stone chasm echoing with
romance and adventure – and
hidden drunks.

"

**Kenneth Slessor (1901–1971), Australian poet,
journalist and war correspondent, writing about
living in Kings Cross in 1923**

In the 1920s, the influx of
cafés, delicatessens, theatres
and nightclubs transformed

Kings Cross

from a well-to-do residential
area into a centre of artistic bohemian
lifestyle that ultimately became
Sydney's seedy red-light district
of today.

> **"**
>
> I've changed Sydney.
> It's my city, my people.
> I'm theirs.
> We belong to each other.
>
> **"**

Harry Triguboff,
Sydney billionaire real-estate developer

The prices for
Sydney real estate are
legendary. In fact, Sydney
prices surpass both
New York and Paris as
the most expensive real
estate in the world.

CHAPTER
SIX

Essential Sydney

The history of a city like Sydney is made up of grand gestures, cultural events, important people and magnificent structures.

However, the glue holding all of those defining moments together is made up of many little stories.

These little stories describe the character, the charm and the essence of Sydney.

Two French navy ships entered Botany Bay a few days after the First Fleet arrived in 1788.

It is often thought that, had the First Fleet been a week late, Australia could have become a French colony.

In 1942 during
World War II, the
pylons of Sydney
Harbour Bridge
were used as
anti-aircraft gun
emplacements.

Essential Slang

Balmain Uppercut: a knee to the groin.

Balmain Fair Go: being attacked from behind with a chair in a pub brawl. Balmain is an innner-city harbour-side suburb where a lot of wharf workers used to live, and pub brawls were said to be common there.

Blind Mullet: untreated faecal matter seen floating on the surface of Sydney Harbour as a result of raw sewage being released into the water. This practice was stopped in the early 1960s when sewage plants were upgraded.

Bondi Cigar: see *Blind Mullet*, except being seen in the surf at Bondi.

Cronulla Cape: to wear the Australian flag tied around the neck, resembling a cape. A reference to the 2005 Cronulla riots that followed an altercation on Cronulla Beach.

The Cross: Kings Cross area of Sydney.

Get off at Redfern: a form of contraception whereby the male withdraws before ejaculation. It refers to Redfern Station being the last train stop before Sydney's Central Station.

The Insular Peninsular: the farthest of the northern beaches area of Sydney from Pittwater to Palm Beach along a thin peninsular of land where, it is said, that residents typically never leave.

Shoot through like a Bondi tram: to exit a situation quickly. The Bondi Express tram was known to speed along suburban streets toward the eastern beaches without stopping.

It's Sydney or the bush: an all-or-nothing proposition.

Southerly Buster: an abrupt southerly breeze change on a hot day that brings strong winds and a dramatic drop in temperature.

Shark Arm Case

In 1935, a captured tiger shark, on display at the Coogee Beach Aquarium Baths, regurgitated a human arm.

Owing to a distinctive tattoo, it was discovered to have belonged to a known missing person. The arm had also been cut off. This fact sparked a murder investigation, but nobody was ever charged.

On hot days
the steel structure of
the Sydney Harbour
Bridge expands,
causing the height of
the arch to increase by
18cm (7.1in).

In 1932, Lennie Gwyther rode his
pony Ginger Mick 1,000km (621 miles)
from his home in southeastern
Victoria to see the opening of the
Sydney Harbour Bridge. On his journey,
he met the Prime Minster of Australia,
his cricketing idol Don Bradman
and the Lord Mayor of Sydney.
He and Ginger Mick also took part in
the bridge-opening pageant!

A remarkable journey indeed,
made even more so by the fact that
Lennie was only nine years old.

Owing to it's actual shape, Circular Quay was originally called "Semi-Circular Quay". The name was shortened for convenience.

In the year Sydney Harbour Bridge was opened, Bridget and Archie were popular baby names.

Paul Hogan,
who played Mick Dundee
in the hit 1986 movie

Crocodile Dundee

worked as a painter
on the Sydney Harbour Bridge
before becoming a famous
TV and movie personality.

It takes around
100 people
every day to maintain
Sydney Harbour
Bridge.

The suburb of Hollywood

in southwest Sydney was developed following the completion of the East Hills railway line in 1931.

However, it didn't always have this name. In 1940, the suburb took the moniker of the famous Californian district because, apparently, the residents didn't like its original name of Dumbleton.

An eclectic playlist featuring Sydney's many facets:

"The Waitress" – The Waifs

"Reckless" – Australian Crawl

"Deep Water" – Richard Clapton

"Breakfast at Sweethearts" – Cold Chisel

"Wedding Cake Island" – Midnight Oil

"Darling It Hurts" – Paul Kelly

"Fast Boat to Sydney" – Johnny Cash &
June Carter Cash

"The Winner Is..." – Southend

"And the Band Played Waltzing Matilda" – The Pogues

"Botany Bay" – Aussie Bush Band

"Chunder in the Old Pacific Sea" – Barry McKenzie

Urban Myth

Martin Plaza, a member of Sydney rock band Mental As Anything, is said to have written their 1979 hit song "The Nips Are Getting Bigger" while driving across the Sydney Harbour Bridge.

As the legend goes, it came to him as he passed through the toll gates on the southern end, and by the time he reached the northern end of the bridge, the song was fully formed in his head.

"

Good evening, and welcome to television.

"

So said Bruce Gyngell on the Nine
Network TV station TCN-9-Sydney
when he launched Australian
mainstream television in 1956.

Doyle's on the Beach

is probably Sydney's most famous
seafood restaurant.

Perched right on the shoreline at
Watsons Bay, diners can enjoy fresh
seafood while taking in the harbour
surrounds.

Doyle's might be known to
serve an expensive fish and chips, but
what a location!

The Fort Denison Prank

In 1900, Charles Lightoller, the fourth officer of White Star Line ship SS *Medic*, decided to prank Sydneysiders into thinking the Boer War had come to town. He and two shipmates rowed to Fort Denison one night, hoisted a Boer flag and fired one of the guns.

He was later transferred to the Atlantic route where, in 1912, he was the most senior officer to survive the sinking of the RMS *Titanic*.

Australia Square is actually round

Built in 1967, Australia Square, at 264 George Street, was the world's tallest lightweight concrete building and, until 1976, Sydney's tallest building.

The cylindrical design, groundbreaking at the time, also means that visitors can dine in the revolving restaurant on the 47th floor.

Crime-wise, in 2019 Sydney was ranked the fifth safest city in the world according to *The Independent* newspaper in Britain.

66

Just where is
Kings Cross? – or, as it is
referred to affectionately by
those who live there – The
Cross. Can anyone say,
or point to it definitely, or
define its boundaries?

99

H.C. Brewster, *Kings Cross Calling* (1954)

In 1999, artist Lynne Roberts-Goodwin created six separate artworks set into sidewalk pavements that trace the path of the Tank Stream from Pitt Street, at Circular Quay, all the way up to Elizabeth Street.

You can follow the course of the stream starting with a plaque in the pavement at the bottom of Pitt Street.

First Flag

On the sidewalk of Loftus Street,
only a few metres from Circular Quay,
you'll find a flagpole flying the Union
Jack. This marks the site where Captain
Arthur Phillip and his men first hoisted
their flag on 26 January 1788.

Depending on who you talk to, this either
marks the establishment of Australia,
or the beginning of the invasion of the
continent by Europeans.

The golden scissors used to cut the ribbons at the Harbour Bridge openings (on both sides of the bridge) were second-hand.

They had been used the year before at the dedication of the Bayonne Bridge linking New Jersey and Staten Island.

On 16 January 1839, the barque *Tartar* entered Sydney Harbour carrying 250 tons of ice cut from a frozen lake near Boston, USA.

For the next 20 summers, Sydneysiders would often escape the heat by sipping on chilled drinks courtesy of the international ice trade.

In 1860, importation was suddenly halted when the Sydney Ice Company began making ice locally.

66

I think that I could never spy
A poem lovely as a pie.
A banquet in a single course
Blushing with rich tomato sauce.

99

Barry Humphries,
Neglected Poems and Other Creatures (1991)

Harry's
Café de Wheels

is a Sydney institution, now firmly grounded near the gates of the Woolloomooloo Naval Yard. But in the early days, this iconic Sydney pie cart needed its wheels because the city council at the time required food vans to move at least 30cm (12in) each day.

At one time, as the legend goes, it was temporarily renamed Café de Axle when the wheels were unfortunately stolen.

Officially, Opera Australia's 1973 production of Prokofiev's *War and Peace* was the first performance in the Sydney Opera House. But American singer and actor Paul Robeson, while on tour in 1960, gave an impromptu concert to the construction workers, thus becoming the first performance in the building.

In the 1879 Sydney Cricket Ground riot, one of the umpires was assaulted by the angry crowd.

The other umpire on the field, who escaped unharmed, was Edmund Barton, who would go on to become Australia's first Prime Minister in 1901.

❝

Sydney is rather like an arrogant lover. When it rains it can deny you its love and you can find it hard to relate to. It's not a place that's built to be rainy or cold. But when the sun comes out, it bats its eyelids, it's glamorous, beautiful, attractive, smart, and it's very hard to get away from its magnetic pull.

❞

Baz Luhrmann, director, writer and producer